D0913008

The Countries

Greece

Tamara L. Britton
ABDO Publishing Company

visit us at
www.abdopub.com

Published by ABDO Publishing Company, 4940 Viking Drive, Suite 622, Edina, Minnesota 55435.
Copyright © 2000 Abdo Consulting Group, Inc., Pentagon Tower, P.O. Box 36036, Minneapolis,
Minnesota 55435 USA. International copyrights reserved in all countries. No part of this book may be
reproduced in any form without written permission from the publisher.

Printed in the United States.

Interior Photos: Corbis, AP Photo Archive
Editors: Bob Italia and Kate A. Furlong
Art Direction & Maps: Pat Laurel
Cover & Interior Design: MacLean & Tuminelly (Mpls.)

Library of Congress Cataloging-in-Publication Data

Britton, Tamara L., 1963-
   Greece / Tamara L. Britton.
      p. cm. -- (The countries)
  Includes index.
  ISBN 1-57765-385-8
  1. Greece--Juvenile literature. [1. Greece.] I. Title. II. Series.

DF717 .B75 2000
949.5--dc21

                                                       00-040589

Contents

Gia'sou!

Greetings from Greece! Greece is an ancient country in Europe. It has mountains, beaches, and many small islands. Its varied land makes Greece home to many kinds of plants and animals.

People have lived in Greece for thousands of years. Greece's people have made contributions to **philosophy**, **architecture**, and medicine.

Greece's **economy** is based on farming and shipping. Greece has one of the world's largest merchant marines. Greece's government is a **parliamentary republic**. Greeks elect the lawmakers. The lawmakers must follow Greece's **constitution**.

Greece has faced many problems in its long history. Wars, **invasions**, a poor economy, and high **unemployment** have challenged the Greek people. Today, Greece is a member of the **European Union (EU)** and is working hard to improve the lives of its citizens.

Gia'sou *from Greece!*

Fast Facts

OFFICIAL NAME: Hellenic Republic (Greece)
CAPITAL: Athens

LAND
- Mountain Ranges: Pindus Mountains
- Highest Point: Mount Olympus 9,570 feet (2,917 m)
- Lowest Point: Sea level
- Major Rivers: Achelos, Vardar, Struma, Nestos

PEOPLE
- Population: 10,707,135 (1999 est.)
- Major Cities: Athens, Thessaloniki
- Language: Greek (official)
- Religion: Greek Orthodox (official)

GOVERNMENT
- Form: Parliamentary Republic
- Head of State: President
- Head of Government: Prime Minister
- Legislature: Unicameral Parliament
- Flag: A white cross in a blue field in the upper mast-side corner, with nine alternating blue and white stripes
- Nationhood: 1829

ECONOMY
- Agricultural Products: Wheat, corn, barley, sugar beets, olives, tomatoes, wine, tobacco, potatoes, beef, dairy products
- Mining Products: Petroleum, natural gas, zinc, salt, silver, copper
- Manufactured Products: Textiles, clothing, food products, chemicals, construction materials, transportation equipment, iron, steel, aluminum
- Money: Drachma

Greece's Flag

A bill worth 1,000 drachma

Timeline

3000 B.C.	Minoans begin first Greek civilization
2000 B.C.	Myceneans live on Peloponnesia
1450 B.C.	Minoan civilization destroyed by earthquake
1193 B.C.	Greeks fight Trojan War against Troy
1100 B.C.	Dorians conquer Greece
490 B.C.	King Darius of Persia attacks Greece
431 B.C.	Peloponnesian War begins
323 B.C.	Romans conquer Greece
A.D. 330	Greece under Byzantine rule
379	Christianity becomes official religion
1054	Byzantine Empire splits into two branches
1453	Ottoman Turks conquer Greece
1821	Archbishop Germanos declares Greece's independence
1829	Greece wins independence from Turkey
1833	Otto I becomes king
1862	King Otto dethroned
1863	George I of Denmark becomes king
1919	Greece attacks Turkey
1936	Metaxas leads military takeover
1944	Civil War begins
1967	Military controls government
1974	Greece becomes a republic
1981	Greece joins the EU

Greece's History

An ancient statue of Zeus from the Cyprus Museum

Ancient Greece was home to many people, including some of history's greatest **scholars**. Many believed in Greek **mythology**. These myths told of a family of gods and goddesses that lived on Mount Olympus. In these myths, Zeus was the most powerful god.

Mythology was the religion of ancient Greece. The first civilization in Greece began around 3,000 B.C. on the island of Crete. It was called the Minoan Civilization after King Minos, who ruled the island. The Minoans had an advanced civilization. They built **elaborate** palaces. Minoan Civilization flourished until 1450 B.C., when it was destroyed by an **earthquake**.

In about 2000 B.C., the Mycenaeans lived in Peloponnesia. There, they built the palace of Mycenae. The entrance to the palace is the famous Lion's Gate.

In 1193 B.C., the Mycenaeans fought in the Trojan War against Troy. The war lasted ten years. The Greeks finally won. The story of the Trojan War is told in Homer's great poems, the *Iliad* and the *Odyssey*.

The Lion's Gate at Mycenae gets its name from the two large lions carved above the doorway.

In 1100 B.C., the Dorians conquered Greece. The Dorians were not as advanced as the Greeks. They could not read or write. But, they had better weapons made of a new material called iron. The Dorian **invasion** began the Dark Ages in Greece.

During this time, Greek **city-states** gained power. These cities were **isolated** from one another by Greece's rugged landscape. Athens, Thebes, Corinth, and Sparta were famous city-states.

In 490 B.C., King Darius of Persia wanted to conquer Greece. He attacked Greece and started the Persian War. But the **city-states** worked together and defeated the Persians. This began the Classical Period in Greek history.

Hippocrates is known as the father of medicine.

During the Classical Period, Perecles ruled Greece. He made Greece a **democracy**. Hippocrates studied medicine. Today, new doctors must take the Hippocratic Oath. Sophocles wrote plays. He invented stage scene **props**. Socrates was a philosopher. He believed ignorance was the root of all evil. Plato was his student. **Scholars** still study Socrates today. Greek **architects** built beautiful temples.

Perecles died in 429 B.C. In 431 B.C., a civil war began in Greece. It is called the Peloponnesian War. Sparta and Athens fought for 28 years. The Spartans won, but the war weakened the Greek city-states. Soon, the Macedonians conquered Greece. Alexander the Great ruled Greece until 323 B.C. Then, the Romans conquered Greece.

The Romans ruled Greece until A.D. 330, when it fell under Byzantine rule. In 379, Christianity became the official religion of Byzantium, and the gods and goddesses of Greek **mythology** were declared evil. Many Greek temples and sculptures were destroyed. In 1054, the Byzantine Empire divided into eastern and western branches. This weakened the once mighty empire and left it open to **invasion**.

Mosaic art was popular in Byzantine Greece. Mosaics are pictures made up of small pieces of colored glass.

In 1453, Ottoman Turks conquered Greece. The Turks were **Muslims**. They made Christians pay high taxes. And Christian families with more than one son had to give up one boy to serve in the Turkish army. The Greek people were unhappy under these conditions. Many left Greece.

The Turks ruled Greece for 400 years. But on March 25, 1821, Archbishop Germanos proclaimed independence for Greece.

France, Britain, and Russia helped the Greeks fight the Turks. In 1829, Greece won its independence.

France, Britain, and Russia set up Greece's new government in 1833. That year, they picked Otto I of Bavaria to be king. Otto was a 17-year-old Roman Catholic. He ruled with absolute power. The Greeks did not want him to be king.

In 1844, there was an **uprising**, and Otto had to

King Otto I

King George I

add a **parliament** and a **prime minister** to the government. But he still did not listen to the people. In 1862, the Greeks **revolted**, and Otto was removed from the throne. George I of Denmark became king in 1863. He ruled until 1913. Then, his son Constantine I became king.

In 1917, Constantine's son George II became king. Greece wanted to gain more territory. In 1918, after World War I, the region of Thrace was added. In 1919, Greece attacked Turkey to get more land. It was a long war. In the end, Greece and Turkey signed a treaty.

In 1920, Constantine I returned to the throne. Then in 1935, George II became king again. In 1936, Johannes Metaxas led a military takeover of Greece. In 1940, during World War II, Benito Mussolini wanted to build military bases in Greece. But Metaxas said no. So, Italy attacked Greece. In 1941, Germany invaded Greece. King George II moved to England and ruled from there.

In 1944, the Germans went to other countries to fight. Soon, another civil war began in Greece. Some Greeks wanted a **monarchy** and some wanted a **communist** government. The war lasted until 1949. The communists lost. In 1964, Constantine II became king.

In 1967, the military took over the government. Military rule lasted until 1974. Then, the Greeks voted to end the monarchy. Greece became a **parliamentary republic**. In 1975, a new **constitution** was adopted. In 1981, Greece joined the **European Union (EU)**.

Today, Greece is a growing country. Its government is stable and its **economy** is improving. The Greek people are looking forward to a promising future.

Greece is a strong country and its people have much national pride.

Greece's Land

Greece is the southernmost country in Europe. It is at the end of the Balkan **Peninsula**. Albania, the Former Yugoslav Republic of Macedonia (FYROM), Bulgaria, and Turkey border

Greece on the north. Greece is surrounded by water on the other three sides. The Mediterranean Sea is on the south. To the east is the Aegean Sea, and to the west is the Ionian Sea.

Greece is divided into three areas. Northern Greece contains the regions of Thrace and Macedonia. This area has cold, harsh winters and cool summers.

Mount Olympus is in the Macedonia region. At 9,570 feet (2,917 m), it is Greece's highest mountain.

Central Greece is made up of the regions of Thessaly, Epirus, and Sterea Ellada. This area has cold winters and hot summers.

Southern Greece contains Attica and Peloponnesia. Peloponnesia is called the Peloponnese. It is a mountainous land mass that extends southward into the Mediterranean Sea. The **Isthmus** of Corinth connects it to the mainland.

Greece is also made up of more than 2,000 islands. The largest is Crete. Crete is mountainous. It has hot, dry summers and mild winters.

The Ionian Islands are in the Ionian Sea. These islands get a lot of rain. The Aegean Islands are in the Aegean Sea. These islands are very dry.

Fields of yellow flowers and olives groves dot Crete's land.

Rainfall

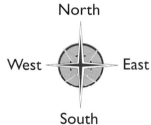

North

West — East

South

AVERAGE YEARLY RAINFALL

Inches		Centimeters
Under 10		*Under 25*
10 - 20		*25 - 50*
20 - 40		*50 - 100*
40 - 60		*100 - 150*
Over 60		*Over 150*

Temperature

Winter

ATHENS ★

Summer

AVERAGE TEMPERATURE

Fahrenheit		Celsius
Over 68°		*Over 20°*
50° - 68°		*10° - 20°*
32° - 50°		*0° - 10°*
Under 32°		*Under 0°*

Plants & Animals

A forest on the island of Rhodes

Greece's varied climate makes it home to many different plants and animals. In northern Greece, there are wildcats, bear, deer, and wolves. There are also lynx and wild boar. Oak, chestnut, and Grecian fir trees grow there.

In the southern region, jackal, wild goats, and porcupine live. Evergreens, shrubs, and leafy plants grow there.

Since Greece is surrounded by water on three sides, pelicans, storks, and herons are plentiful. In the winter, many birds come to Greece where it is warm.

A pair of storks stand beak-to-beak in their nest in Lesbos.

Mountain goats stand on a cliff in Cephalonia, the largest of the Ionian Islands.

The Greeks

Most of the people that live in Greece are Greeks. But some Turks, Albanians, Gypsies, and Jews live there, too. Greece is a mixture of all its people's **cultures**.

The Greek Alphabet		
LETTER NAME	UPPERCASE	LOWERCASE
Alpha	A	α
Beta	B	β
Gamma	Γ	γ
Delta	Δ	δ
Episilon	E	ε
Zeta	Z	ζ
Eta	H	η
Theta	Θ	θ
Iota	I	ι
Kappa	K	κ
Lambda	Λ	λ
Mu	M	μ
Nu	N	ν
Xi	Ξ	ξ
Omicron	O	ο
Pi	Π	π
Rho	P	ρ
Sigma	Σ	σ
Tau	T	τ
Upsilon	Y	υ
Phi	Φ	φ
Chi	X	χ
Psi	Ψ	ψ
Omega	Ω	ω

Greek is the official language in Greece. It is the oldest language spoken in Europe. Greece uses a unique alphabet. It has 24 letters. The English alphabet has 26 letters. It is possible to write Greek using English letters. For example, the word *lunch* written in Greek using the English alphabet is *mesimeriano*. The word *lunch* written using the Greek alphabet is μεσημεριανο.

The official religion in Greece is Greek Orthodox. Before the Byzantine Empire split into two branches in 1054, the Eastern Orthodox and Roman Catholic churches were one body. After the split, Greek Orthodox evolved from the Eastern Orthodox Church.

Greek families are very close. Families are made up of a husband, wife, and their unmarried children. Children live with their parents until they get married. Sometimes, a newly married couple will live with the husband's family until they can afford their own house.

In the cities, many Greeks live in high-rise apartment buildings. In the rural areas, houses made of brick have wooden floors. They are painted with a kind of paint called **whitewash**.

Greek weddings are family celebrations. First, there is a church ceremony. Then, guests attend parties.

Whitewashed houses look bright against the blue sea.

Greek families enjoy many unique foods. *Moussaka* is a casserole of layered eggplant and ground meat in a rich sauce. *Dolmathes* are grape leaves stuffed with rice and ground meat. And everybody loves *baklava*, a dessert made of pastry and nuts soaked in honey.

Greek children must go to school for nine years. Books and tuition are free. At age six, children begin elementary school. It is called *demotiko*.

Next, students go to *gymnasio* for three years. The last three years of Greek school are called *lycio*. After *lycio*, students may go on to a university if they pass the admission tests. At the university, tuition, books, room, and board are all free.

After they complete their schooling, Greeks work in many different jobs. They are farmers, government workers, hotel managers, sailors, teachers, and many other professions.

Demotiko *students participate in gym class.*

Tzatziki

Tzatziki is a popular side dish in Greece. It can be used as a sauce for gyro sandwiches, a dip for chips and vegetables, or even as a salad dressing!

1 cup plain yogurt
2-3 tbsp. olive oil
1 tsp. dill weed
3-4 cloves minced garlic
1 cucumber, peeled, seeded, and chopped

Stir all ingredients together in a bowl. Refrigerate for 1 hour. Add salt and pepper to taste.

AN IMPORTANT NOTE TO THE CHEF: Always have an adult help with the preparation and cooking of food. Never use kitchen utensils or appliances without adult permission and supervision.

LANGUAGE

ENGLISH	GREEK
Thank You	Efharisto'
Mother	Mite'ra
Father	Pate'ras
Hello	Gia'sou
Goodbye	Andi'o
Please	Parakalo'
Yes	Nai
No	Ochi

Money Matters

A woman harvests grapes by hand.

Greece is one of the poorest **EU** countries. It **imports** twice as much as it **exports**.

Greece is a dry country with poor soil. Less than a third of the land can be farmed. But a third of all Greeks are farmers. They manage to grow grapes, olives, and vegetables in the challenging soil.

Greece has few natural resources. Coal, bauxite, and lignite are mined.

Tourism is Greece's largest **industry**. More than 11 million people visit Greece each year. There are many hotels, restaurants, and shops to serve the tourists. More Greeks work in the **hospitality** industry than any other.

Thousands of tourists visit the Parthenon in Athens every year. The ancient Greeks completed the Parthenon in 432 B.C. It is a temple dedicated to Athena, the goddess of war.

Greece's Beautiful Cities

The capital of Greece is Athens. It is Greece's largest city. About 1 million people live there. It was named after the Greek goddess Athena. Athens is dominated by the Acropolis, a flat-topped hill in the center of the city.

During Greece's Classical Period, the Acropolis was the city's **cultural** center. Its most famous building is the Parthenon, the temple of Athena. The Propylaea, the Erechtheum, the Theater of Dionysus, and the Odeum of Perecles are also on the Acropolis. The Odeum is still used for theater performances today.

The buildings on the Acropolis have examples of Greek **architecture**. Doric architecture uses plain columns. Ionic uses columns decorated with scrolls, and Corinthian has columns decorated with acanthus leaves.

A Doric column

An Ionic column

A Corinthian column

Athens is the **economic** center of Greece. All of Greece's regions and major cities are connected to Athens by roads and railroads.

Industry in Athens accounts for almost half of Greece's economy. People build ships, mill flour, and make paper and textiles. Other products are glass, tiles, bricks, soap, and chemicals.

There are many museums in Athens. The national museum and the Acropolis Museum have many collections of art and antiquities. The Byzantine Museum, the National Gallery of Art, and the National Library are also in Athens.

The National Capodistrain University of Athens was founded in 1837. Athens also has a technical university, two business colleges, a teacher training college, and the Academy of Science.

The Parthenon rises from the Acropolis in Athens.

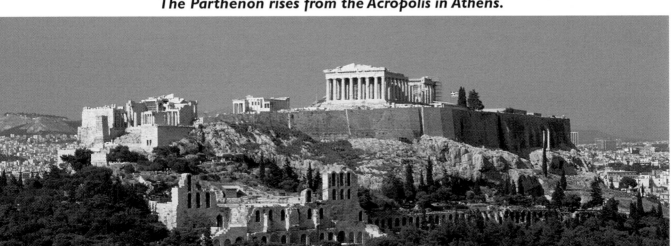

Thessaloniki is Greece's second-largest city. About 400,000 people live there. It was named after Alexander the Great's sister.

The port in Thessaloniki is second only to Piraeus's in size. The city is linked to other areas of Greece and the Balkans by roads and railroads. These things make Thessaloniki an important center of commerce for Greece and the Balkans.

Thessaloniki **exports** chrome, manganese, and agricultural products. Other **industries** include **petroleum** products, textiles, bricks, soap, and flour.

Thessaloniki is the seat of the Greek Orthodox Church. It has a university, an American school, and a French school.

A variety of olives are displayed in a Thessaloniki market.

Piraeus is Greece's third-largest city. About 170,000 people live there. Its port is the largest in Greece. It is the center of Greece's sea transportation. Chemicals, machinery, textiles, and ships are produced there, too.

Greeks have used Piraeus's port since ancient times.

Greece on the Go

A ship sails through the Corinth Canal.

Since Greece is almost entirely surrounded by the sea, water transportation is very important. Greece has three main ports. Piraeus, the port of Athens, handles more than half of Greece's shipping. Thessaloniki is the port used for other Balkan countries. Patras is the main port on the Peloponnese. Ferries connect it to the mainland and Italy.

The Corinth Canal connects the Ionian Sea to the Aegean Sea. Greece has one of the world's largest merchant marines. Shipping makes a major contribution to Greece's **economy**.

Trains transport many of Greece's products. Construction of railroads began in the 1880s. There are about 1,000 miles (1,609 km) of both standard- and narrow-gauge tracks. Currently, Greece is working to modernize its railway system.

There are about 73,000 miles (117,000 km) of roads in Greece. Almost all of them are paved. Many Greeks travel by car. This has overloaded Greece's roadway system. Greece has more car accidents than any other European country. In Athens, more than 500,000 cars crowd the city. It is one of Europe's most polluted cities. Often, Athens is covered with a white cloud of smog. The smog is very harmful to the buildings on the Acropolis.

Airplanes transport people into and out of Greece. The national airline is Olympic Airways. Greece's main airports are Ellinikon in Athens and Macedonia in Thessaloniki.

Heavy traffic in Athens

Greece's Government

Greece's government is a **parliamentary republic**. It follows the **constitution** of 1975. The powers of the government are divided into three branches: executive, legislative, and judicial.

In the executive branch, the president is the head of state. The **prime minister** is the head of government. The prime minister leads the majority party in **parliament** and sets government policies. There is also a **cabinet** that is selected by the prime minister and appointed by the president.

The legislative branch consists of a 300-member parliament. The parliament is unicameral. This means that there are no upper and lower houses. Each member of parliament has one equal vote. Parliamentary elections occur every four years.

Greek soldiers called evzoni *guard the parliament building.*

The judicial branch is made up of civil, criminal, and administrative courts. The lower courts are responsible for minor civil and criminal cases. There are 12 Courts of Appeal. The Supreme Court hears appeals from the Courts of Appeal. The Special Supreme Tribunal hears cases involving **parliamentary** election **disputes**, and disputes between courts and government agencies.

On the local level, Greece's nine regions are divided into 52 **provinces**. Each province has a governor, who serves as the link between local and central government.

A meeting of the Greek parliament

Festivals & Holidays

On January 1, Greeks celebrate St. Basil's day. This is a festive time of parties and gift giving. Five days later, Greeks celebrate **Epiphany**. Priests bless seas, lakes, and rivers. Children participate in Epiphany festivities, such as parades.

March 25 is Independence Day in Greece. This celebrates Greece's independence from Turkey.

One of the most celebrated holidays in Greece is Easter. The celebration begins with Carnival. Everyone eats and drinks a lot to prepare for **Lent**.

Children dressed in traditional Greek clothing walk in an Epiphany parade.

Greek baked goods made for Easter celebrations

During the 40 days of **Lent**, **devout** Greeks do not consume meat, olive oil, or wine. On Easter Sunday, a special church service is held. A large Easter dinner follows the service.

During the Easter service at a Greek Orthodox church, people go to the altar and light candles.

Most Greeks celebrate "name day" instead of their birthday. On the **feast day** of the saint that they are named after, Greeks have a party for their friends.

October 28 is *Ochi* Day. *Ochi* means "no" in Greek. This holiday celebrates the night in 1940 that Johannes Metaxas said no to Benito Mussolini's demand to build military bases in Greece.

Sports & Leisure

Many Greek kids like to play soccer.

Soccer is the most popular sport in Greece. Greece has a professional league made up of 16 teams. Greece also competes in international competitions. Basketball is also popular.

The Olympic games began in ancient times on the Peloponnese in Olympia. In 1896, the first modern Olympics were held in Athens. Olympic competition returns to Greece when Athens hosts the 2004 summer games.

Greeks also like to listen to music. They listen to classical, jazz, and rock. But many Greeks prefer **traditional** music played on a *bouzouki*. A *bouzouki* is a stringed instrument that looks like a mandolin. *Rebetika* is a traditional style of music played on a *bouzouki*.

A bouzouki *player*

Greeks like to attend the theater. There are more than 100 theaters in Athens. In rural areas, there are outdoor theaters that are thousands of years old. Television is a popular pastime, too.

The Greek lifestyle and activities reflect its colorful **culture**. For thousands of years Greece has contributed to the world with its art, **democracy**, and **philosophy**. Though Greece faces **economic** challenges, its people look forward to a bright future.

The Theater at Epidaurus seats 14,000 people. But the sound is so good that even people in the last row can hear a pin dropped on stage. Plays are still staged there today.

Glossary

architecture - the art of planning and designing buildings.
cabinet - a group of advisors.
city-state - a state consisting of a city and its surrounding territory.
communism - an economic system in which everything is owned by the government and given to people as they need it.
constitution - a paper that describes a country's laws and government.
culture - the customs, arts, and tools of a people or nation.
democracy - a kind of government where people hold the power. They are represented by elected officials.
devout - religious; active in worship and prayer.
dispute - an angry argument.
earthquake - a trembling or shaking of the ground.
economy - the way a country uses its money, goods, and natural resources.
elaborate - something with many details that is made with great care.
Epiphany - in eastern churches, the celebration of the baptism of Christ.
European Union (EU) - an organization of European countries that works toward political, economic, governmental, and social unity.
export - to send goods to another country to sell or trade.
feast day - a periodic religious ceremony celebrating a saint.
hospitality - operating hotels, motels, and restaurants for tourists.
import - to bring in goods from another country to sell or trade.
industry - the production of a large number of goods by businesses and factories.
invasion - the entrance of armed forces into a country in order to attack it.
isolated - to be separated from something.
isthmus - a narrow strip of land connecting two larger land areas.
Lent - the forty days before Easter.
monarchy - a government ruled by a king, queen, or emperor.
Muslim - one who follows Islam. Islam is a religion based on the teachings of Mohammed as they appear in the Koran.
mythology - a legend or story that attempts to account for something in nature.
parliament - an assembly that makes the laws of a country.
peninsula - land that sticks out into water and is connected to a larger land mass.
petroleum - a thick, yellowish-black oil. It is the source of gasoline.

philosophy - a field of study that attempts to understand the nature of knowledge and reality.

prime minister - the chief official in certain kinds of governments.

prop - in a play, a big picture on a stage that makes the stage look like a certain location.

province - one of the main divisions of a country.

republic - a form of government in which authority rests with voting citizens and is carried out by elected officials such as a parliament.

revolt - when citizens rise up and challenge a government's authority.

scholar - a person that has a lot of knowledge.

tourism - touring or traveling for pleasure. A person traveling for pleasure is called a tourist.

traditional - something that has been passed down through generations.

unemployment - lack of employment, also, the number of people in a country that do not have jobs.

uprising - a revolt.

whitewash - a liquid made of lime and water used for painting.

Web Sites

CIA: World Factbook — Greece
http://www.cia.gov/cia/publications/factbook/gr.html
This site by the CIA offers up-to-date statistics on Greece. It has sections on Greece's geography, people, government, economy, communications, transportation, and military.

Ancient Olympic Games Virtual Museum
http://devlab.cs.dartmouth.edu/olympic/
This site by Dartmouth College has a virtual museum of the ancient Olympics. Learn about the history of the games, the game site, the original contests, the victors, and much more!

These sites are subject to change. Go to your favorite search engine and type in "Greece" for more sites.

Index